TRAIN YOUR MEMORY

Books in the Penguin Pocket Series

THE AUSTRALIAN CALORIE COUNTER
THE AUSTRALIAN EASY SPELLER
AUSTRALIAN GARDENING CALENDER
CASSEROLES FOR FAMILY AND FRIENDS
CHAIRING AND RUNNING MEETINGS
CHESS MADE EASY
CHOOSING A NAME FOR YOUR BABY
CHOOSING AUSTRALIAN WINES
THE COMPACT GUIDE TO WRITING LETTERS
FAMILY FIRST AID
GABRIEL GATÉ'S FAST PASTA
GABRIEL GATÉ'S FAVOURITE FAST RECIPES
GABRIEL GATÉ'S ONE-DISH DINNERS
GOOD FOOD FOR BABIES AND TODDLERS
HOW TO MAKE OVER 200 COCKTAILS
HOW TO PLAY MAH JONG
JULIE STAFFORD'S FAT, FIBRE & ENERGY COUNTER
JULIE STAFFORD'S JUICING BOOK
MICROWAVE MEALS IN MINUTES
MICROWAVE TIPS AND TECHNIQUES
THE PENGUIN POCKET BOOK OF ETIQUETTE
THE PENGUIN POCKET BOOK OF QUOTATIONS
PLAYING CASINO GAMES TO WIN
THE POCKET AUSSIE FACT BOOK
THE POCKET MUFFIN BOOK
THE POCKET WOK COOKBOOK
REMOVING STAINS
SPEAKING IN PUBLIC
TRAINING YOUR MEMORY
USING YOUR NOODLES
WEDDING ETIQUETTE
YOUR NEW BABY

TRAINING YOUR MEMORY

Jonathan Crabtree-Morton

Penguin Books

Penguin Books Australia Ltd
487 Maroondah Highway, PO Box 257
Ringwood, Victoria 3134, Australia
Penguin Books Ltd
Harmondsworth, Middlesex, England
Penguin Putnam Inc.
375 Hudson Street, New York, New York 10014, USA
Penguin Books Canada Limited
10 Alcorn Avenue, Toronto, Ontario, Canada M4V 3B2
Penguin Books (NZ) Ltd
Cnr Rosedale and Airborne Roads, Albany, Auckland, New Zealand
Penguin Books (South Africa) (Pty) Ltd
5 Watkins Street, Denver Ext 4, 2094, South Africa
Penguin Books India (P) Ltd
11, Community Centre, Panchsheel Park, New Delhi 110 017, India

First published by Penguin Books Australia Ltd 1996
This edition published by Penguin Books Australia Ltd 2000

10 9 8 7 6 5 4 3 2

Copyright © Penguin Books Australia Ltd 1996

All rights reserved. Without limiting the rights under copyright reserved above, no part of this publication may be reproduced, stored in or introduced into a retrieval system, or transmitted, in any form or by any means (electronic, mechanical, photocopying, recording or otherwise), without the prior written permission of both the copyright owner and the above publisher of this book.

Material in this book originally appeared in *Improve Your Memory* by Jonathan Crabtree-Morton, published by Penguin Books Australia Ltd, 1990.

Cover design by Anita Bacic, Penguin Design Studio
Cover photography by Igor Sapina
Typeset by Post Pre-press Group, Brisbane, Queensland
Printed in Australia by Australian Print Group, Maryborough, Victoria

National Library of Australia
Cataloguing-in-Publication data:

Crabtree-Morton, Jonathan.
  Training your memory.

  ISBN 0 14 029743 X.

  1. Memory. 2. Mnemonics. I. Crabtree-Morton, Jonathan. Improve your memory. II. Title: Improve your memory.

153.14

www.penguin.com.au

CONTENTS

INTRODUCTION		vii
1	HOW'S YOUR MEMORY?	1
2	YOUR AMAZING BRAIN	11
3	A BRAIN OWNER'S GUIDE	25
4	THE BRAIN CHAIN	36
5	NAMES AND FACES	59
6	YOUR MENTAL FILING CABINET	71
7	OVERCOMING ABSENT-MINDEDNESS	91
8	NUMBER-MUNCHING	96
9	USE IT AND IMPROVE IT	109

INTRODUCTION

Would you like to develop a remarkable memory in just five minutes? You would? Well, forget it! The powerful memory techniques you will find in this book will take a few hours to master before you reap the benefit. Then, with practice, they will become yours for life.

What you will discover is that it is comparatively easy to get results from these special mental exercises. You can, and will, markedly improve your memory skills with surprisingly little effort.

I suggest you do the memory quizzes in Chapter 1 to determine how good your memory is right now. From there you will discover something about your brain's potential; learn how your brain works; become more confident with others as you use effective trigger techniques for remembering names, numbers, addresses, faces, events, and tasks to be done; learn how to enhance your powers of observation; and become more aware of how to maintain your brain as you develop a programme for lifelong memory efficiency.

So, before we begin, have ready a notepad, pen, and watch or clock to time yourself, and be prepared to be surprised!

HOW'S YOUR MEMORY?

Before you begin your memory training it's wise to develop an understanding of how good or poor your untrained memory is. The tests on the following pages will no doubt stretch you to your limits. You may even become a little depressed with your results, yet you can rest assured that by the time you've worked your way through this book such practical exercises will be easy and enjoyable!

Before you start, make sure you have a watch or clock handy so that you can time yourself.

HISTORY TEST: PART 1

TAKE 4 MINUTES TO LEARN THE FOLLOWING EVENTS FROM HISTORY

1942 the first computer was developed

1903 the year of the Wright brothers' first flight

1784 the first daily newspaper was published

1770 the year of Beethoven's birth

1642 Tasmania was discovered

1926 television was first demonstrated

1815 Napoleon lost the battle of Waterloo

1801 the first submarine was built

1969 people landed on the moon

1901 the Nobel prizes were first awarded

Wait 5 minutes, then turn to page 6 and complete the test.

APPOINTMENTS TEST: PART 1

TAKE 2 MINUTES TO MEMORISE THE FOLLOWING THINGS TO DO.

3.00 pm	buy some butter
6.00 pm	fill out a tax form
8.15 am	go on a bicycle ride
2.00 pm	make an important phone call
4.30 pm	pick up a hearing aid for a relative
1.00 pm	visit the dentist
7.00 am	catch a bus
10.00 pm	watch the cricket highlights on television
9.00 am	buy a handbag at the local shops
5.30 pm	turn on an electric radiator

Wait 5 minutes, then turn to page 7 and complete the test.

How's Your Memory?

SHOPPING LIST TEST: PART 1

TAKE 3 MINUTES TO MEMORISE THE TWENTY ITEMS BELOW, DOING YOUR BEST TO RECALL THEM IN THE CORRECT ORDER.

cat food	some fish	television
bananas	window cleaner	fireworks
dinner setting	ice cube tray	soup
meat pie	flea collar	underwear
mouthwash	glass bottle	polish
toilet paper	book	hammer
bunch of flowers	toy train	

Wait 5 minutes before you discover how much you would have bought at the shops, and how much you would have had to go back for! Turn to page 8 to complete the test.

TELEPHONE NUMBER TEST: PART 1

TAKE 10 MINUTES TO LEARN THE FOLLOWING PHONE NUMBERS.

pizza parlour	74 1570	vet	235 9214
kindergarten	327 0605	library	95 7851
plumber	018 49 4715	doctor	82 1195
post office	351 8540	garage	749 1920
police station	41 5131	supermarket	840 4532

Wait 5 minutes, then turn to page 9 and complete the test.

ABSTRACT ITEM PAIRING TEST: PART 1

TAKE 2 MINUTES TO MEMORISE THE FOLLOWING PAIRS OF LETTERS AND NUMBERS.

0 s, 1 t, 2 n, 3 m, 4 r, 5 L, 6 sh, 7 k, 8 f, 9 p.

Wait 5 minutes, then turn to page 10 and complete the test.

HISTORY TEST: PART 2

GIVE THE DATE FOR EACH HISTORICAL EVENT LISTED BELOW.

- *Tasmania was discovered*
- *the first daily newspaper was published*
- *the Nobel prizes were first awarded*
- *the first submarine was built*
- *the year of the Wright brothers' first flight*
- *television was first demonstrated*
- *people landed on the moon*
- *the first computer was developed*
- *the year of Beethoven's birth*
- *Napoleon lost the Battle of Waterloo*

Turn back to page 2 for the answers. Give yourself 2 marks for every correct answer, 1 mark if you get within two years of the correct date. The maximum score is 20.

MY SCORE: __11__ MARKS

APPOINTMENTS TEST: PART 2

GIVE THE TASK TO BE DONE FOR EACH TIME LISTED BELOW.

- ✓ 7.00 am — catch bus
- ✓ 8.15 am — bike ride
- ✓✗ 9.00 am — buy handbag @ local shops.
- ✗ 1.00 pm — make an important phone call
- ✗ 2.00 pm — dentist
- ✓ 3.00 pm — get some pfalse teeth for relative
- ✗ 4.30 pm — buy butter
- ✓ 5.30 pm — turn radiator on
- ✗ 6.00 pm —
- ✓ 10.00 pm — watch cricket highlights

Turn back to page 3 for the answers. Give yourself 1 mark for every correct answer. The maximum score is 10.

MY SCORE: __6__ MARKS

How's Your Memory?

SHOPPING LIST TEST: PART 2

LIST THE TWENTY SHOPPING ITEMS BELOW, IN THE CORRECT ORDER IF POSSIBLE.

cat food / ~~jelly~~
banana / bottle
dinner setting / _____
meat pie / _____
mouth wash / tv
_____ / fireworks
_____ / soap
sore fist / underpants
window cleaner / polish
ice cube tray / hammer

Turn back to page 4 for the answers. Give yourself 1 mark for every correct answer. The maximum score is 20.

MY SCORE: 15 MARKS

TELEPHONE NUMBER TEST: PART 2

GIVE THE PHONE NUMBER FOR EACH PLACE LISTED BELOW.

doctor _____ *supermarket* _____

library _____ *plumber* _____

kindergarten _____ *pizza parlour* _____

garage _____ *post office* _____

vet _____ *police station* _____

Turn back to page 5 for the answers. Give yourself 1 mark for every correct number, and a bonus mark if it matched the right place. The maximum score is 20.

MY SCORE: ___2___ MARKS

ABSTRACT ITEM PAIRING TEST: PART 2

COMPLETE THE PAIRS BY GIVING THE LETTERS FOR EACH NUMBER LISTED BELOW.

6 ½h 4 ƒ 3 m 8 J 5 L 1 t 7 ls 9 p 2 ∩ 0 s

Turn back to page 5 for the answers. Give yourself 1 mark for every correct answer. The maximum score is 10.

MY SCORE: __9__ MARKS

MY TOTAL SCORE: __43__ MARKS

Adding up your marks for the six tests will give you a total score out of 90. Regardless of how you went in these tests (many people fail dismally), I **strongly** suggest you sign the following contract with yourself.

I __KARIM MERELI__ (your name)

will discipline myself and train my mind daily for the next

eight weeks to achieve the memory skills I want in my life.

Date __3/25/04__

Signed _____

YOUR AMAZING BRAIN

I'd like to share with you some rather fascinating ideas about your brain and what it is capable of doing.

Did you know that you have a huge number of brain cells? One estimate is between twelve and fourteen billion cells. The honeybee has only a tiny percentage of the brain cells a human has – about seven thousand – yet some bees can fly for kilometres without getting lost, returning to the same flower at the same time on successive days. Those bees build hives, breed and collect and store honey with a relatively minuscule number of brain cells. The human embryo grows several thousand brain cells in a matter of just three seconds. Can you begin to comprehend the brain power that you have acquired, compared with that of some animals that get by with as few as twenty-five cells?

We often compare the brain with technology. The ancient Greeks, for example, thought that the blood flowed throughout the different parts of the body and was cooled down by the brain (acting somewhat like a car radiator) before going back to the body. Later, people likened the brain to a lump of clay, with memories etched on it, and some thought that's why the brain is all wrinkled like a rockmelon. Then came the idea that the brain was somehow like a factory, with information going in through eyes, nose, mouth, or ears, or the skin, to be processed, sorted and stored in one particular part of the brain.

A more recent concept is that the brain is like a telephone exchange; yet even that analogy is out of date. We now know that the world's entire telecommunication needs – all the computer transmissions, all the faxes, all the telephone calls required throughout the whole world – could be handled by a piece of your brain the size of a walnut.

The current analogy is with the computer. Again, recent estimates have shown that the brain is vastly superior to anything electronic ever built. If a computer were to be built to be a match for your brain, that computer would have to be fifty floors high and cover hundreds of square kilometres! A few years ago when one of the world's most sophisticated computers was pitted against world chess champion Gary Kasparov, it was no match for a human brain. Even though the computer, known as Deep Thought, was able to analyse almost three-quarters of a million positions per second, the computer lost the first game in fifty-seven moves and the second in only thirty-seven moves. A recent rematch also resulted in Kasparov winning – but by a much narrower margin, the computer actually winning a game.

Perhaps you've heard the saying that the average person only uses about one-tenth of his or her mental potential. Scientists and neurologists actually estimate that an untrained mind uses less than 1 per cent of its potential. And I'm not talking about psychic powers or extrasensory perception (ESP), but about demonstrable abilities to learn and remember information.

Each brain cell looks a little like a starfish or an octopus, consisting of a central nucleus surrounded by 'messenger wires' that communicate with other brain cells. More specifically, the outgoing messages flow along fibres called axons, while the incoming messages are received by fibres known as dendrites. While the dendrites are usually less than a millimetre long, the axons can be up to a metre long. If just one of your brain cells were enlarged to the size of a cricket ball, the axons and dendrites connected to it would fill the Sydney Opera House!

Your brain is similar in some respects to a muscle.

The more you use it the bigger it grows. While no new brain cells are formed after birth, every time you concentrate and stretch your mental abilities, your brain sprouts new axons and more interconnections are formed between the different parts of your brain. Einstein's brain cells were said to have had significantly more interconnections than the norm. And, yes, the more you use your brain by keeping mentally active, the more your brain will weigh. Elderly rats in laboratories have experienced an increase in brain weight of the order of 10 per cent after having toys and running wheels to play with!

By the time we reach eighty years of age, even if we lose many thousands of brain cells daily, we will still have more than 90 per cent of the brain cells we had in our youth. You can't run out of space, either: you are capable of absorbing 1000 bits of information per second for 100 years without 'filling up' your brain.

These facts are one of the things that have motivated me to improve my memory. I've also been excited by the extent to which others have been able to improve their memory. When you improve your memory, for practical purposes you become more effective and live your life more intensely. If you lived a life without memory, you would not have *experienced* life. The more powerful your memory the more you enjoy life, too.

Your Belief System

While much emphasis has been placed on the various 'systems' in the body, such as the digestive system, the reproductive system or the central nervous system, the most important system that determines who you are and what you are capable of is your belief system. It's quite likely that through a combination of life experiences and other people's insensitivity, your belief system has taken quite a beating in the area of learning and memory.

For example, when I was a child at primary school my teacher once asked me in class what four times three was. As I began to answer she said, 'Concentrate and look at me! The answer's not on the ceiling!' Needless to say I became flustered and gave the wrong answer, for which I was promptly told that I was stupid at maths, and I swallowed it hook, line and sinker. Who was I to argue? She was the expert. So through a combination of the snickering of the rest of the class and the 'fact' that she was the expert, I brought into my belief system the suggestion that I was stupid at maths.

In a very interesting experiment, a teacher told her young class that all children with blue or light-coloured eyes are smarter than children with dark or brown eyes. Quite quickly the performance in the classroom began to back up her statement. A few weeks later the teacher came into the classroom and apologised for making a mistake.

All babies are born with blue or light-coloured eyes, she said, and as they grow up some get darker eyes, and they're the smarter ones. Just as before, the performance of the children began to become determined by the colour of their eyes. The dark-eyed children 'became smarter' and the children with light-coloured eyes began to fall behind.

In a similar experiment, two different school classes were given an aptitude test to determine how 'smart' they were. They were told that if they did well they would be given a high locker number, while if they didn't do too well they would be given a low locker number. In reality this was really only done with one of the classes. In the other they reversed the rule and gave the 'slower' children a high locker number while the 'brighter' ones were actually given a low locker number. Within a few months, regardless of how good the children were at their schoolwork before the test, their results indicated a correlation between performance and their locker number.

You might think that you're 'all grown up now' and that your belief system isn't as easily bruised as it once was, and yet you'd be wrong. For example, forgetting the name of your boss, as you introduce him or her before a speech, will bruise your belief system enough for you to begin to notice how many names you forget, and from then on you may well expect to forget them – and find that you do.

When I first began teaching memory skills, occasionally

I saw people experience such terrific and rapid changes in their abilities that their belief systems couldn't adapt to their new reality, and consequently the results were only short-lived.

So before you go on to develop your memory I think it's a good idea for me to teach you how to forget. You see, unless you systematically dismantle any negative beliefs that you have regarding your mental skills, the habits of a lifetime won't be too easily changed. So now is a good time to learn the 'Five-minute Fear Fix'.

THE FIVE-MINUTE FEAR FIX

Think back to a powerful yet negative experience you have had in your life in the area of learning and memory. It might be arguing over homework with parents, getting a bad report card, being embarrassed in class in front of others, being told you're stupid by a teacher or any one of dozens of unpleasant experiences. (The one I started with was the memory of struggling through and failing a chemistry exam.)

We will now lessen the influence this experience may be having in your life. In a way, we will be doing some mental gardening. If left untended over the years, your fertile imagination will have grown a large crop of mental weeds! If, for example, you once received a horrendous report card, you may believe, either consciously or subconsciously, that all future results will be like this, and as a result always avoid any situations in which there's a chance you may 'fail'. (Failure, by the way, is simply feedback. If you 'failed' the tests in Chapter 1, all it means is that you will benefit from the ideas in this book.)

Firstly, while you follow the steps for weeding negative memories from your mind, click the thumb and forefinger on your non-writing hand together once, leaving your thumb and forefinger touching. This will become a mental security blanket that allows you to contemplate negative memories without reinforcing them.

Next, to increase the flow of blood to your neocortex (the grey matter of your brain), stimulate neuro-vascular pressure points on your forehead. (*Neuro* is the descriptive form of *neuron*, a nerve, while *vascular* describes blood flow in the veins.) To do this, with your eyes closed cup your writing hand slightly, place it on your forehead and flatten your hand so that the skin of your forehead is stretched very slightly. You may have noticed that people often bring a hand to their forehead when they are trying to think or remember something; they are subconsciously stimulating the flow of blood to their brain. Now take yourself through the following steps.

1 For about 30 seconds, contemplate any sights, sounds or feelings associated with your negative memory.

2 Fade out all the colour from this memory so that it becomes a boring, monochrome movie.
3 Lower and then turn off all the volume in your mind so that you now have a black and white film with no sound.
4 Feel yourself looking back on the experience as you walk away from it. Become aware of your footsteps getting fainter and the size of the memory getting smaller.

It's likely your arm will have become a little tired, so relax as I briefly explain what you just did.

Negative experiences are usually emotionally disturbing, embedded in the memory and long lasting. Have you ever woken up from a nightmare finding your heart racing, your face flushed and sweaty, and feeling really bad? Your body has been reacting physically to imagined experiences, as the mind often doesn't know the difference between an imagined experience and a 'real' experience.

My natural tendency in the past was to repeat and therefore reinforce negative experiences with some regularity. Are you the same? For example, I was once a very nervous speaker. The first time I had to read aloud in school was a disaster. As a result, from that moment I tried to avoid public speaking, just in case the sight of people's faces about to burst into laughter made me feel sick to the stomach again. I carried the belief that I was a poor speaker around as 'excess baggage' for years, until it dawned on me that the only way I could become a success as a mind and memory trainer was to become an entertaining and informative public speaker.

I went over the process of dismantling the memory of my poor performance as a public speaker as you have just done. I faded out the colour so that mocking faces didn't have much power any more. I turned the volume down, with the next screening of the memory, so that I wouldn't fear the sound of laughter again. Then I imagined walking away from the experience, being aware of an increasing feeling of satisfaction flowing through my feet. As I mentally walked away from the silent black and white experience, it also became smaller and smaller. That helped me put things back into proportion. All too often we tend to 'make a mountain out of a molehill' and exaggerate the situation. The distancing technique will help you feel more in control, and prevent you from getting into a spiral of negative self-talk.

Now we have done some mental weeding, it's important to plant some fruit, otherwise mental weeds – in the form of faulty beliefs – are sure to grow back. In the process that follows I want you to become a mental movie producer. You will have at your disposal the greatest script that you can have, sensurround, odorama and superb hi-fi sound. You will also be the star performer, giving the performance of your life.

Are you ready to rehearse your new performance in the area of your life that you wish to improve? You are? Good! Start off with a smile. This actually alters your heart and breathing rate and lowers the temperature of your blood before it gets to your brain, making you feel better.

Click your thumb and forefinger again, and restimulate the neuro-vascular pressure points on your forehead. (Interestingly, these are also known to be emotional stress release points.) Then take yourself through the following steps.

1 Return to the experience you dismantled, and totally change the imagery so that things could not possibly look better. If there were angry or upset people in the experience, let them now have big, beaming smiles. If before you looked awkward and clumsy, now see yourself as vibrant and graceful.
2 For the next minute, close your eyes and continue to picture the situation with those perfect sights, and begin to turn up the colour until it becomes almost fluorescent.
3 Tune in, and turn up your inner volume, with all the sounds absolutely perfect. Birds may be singing,

people are saying lovely things about you, and you sound happy and confident.

4. Think of the positive outcomes you will experience when these things you are visualising become true. This time I suggest that, as well as having perfect sights and sounds, you imagine that you have just succeeded and feel absolutely thrilled! (At this stage in my example, I contemplated the feeling of just receiving the results of my chemistry exam, and being awarded a high distinction. In my mind I was now being offered a lecturing position at Oxford University. Wow! The thought of this excited me to such an extent that I felt butterflies in my chest.) Make sure that you exaggerate the feelings of success that you will soon experience in this part of your life.

Congratulations! I hope that felt good. You have just dismantled that negative memory piece by piece and inserted a powerful new experience in its place. Of course you will still be able to remember the initial memory, but you'll find that now it won't make you upset or prevent you from achieving your goals, as it may have in the past.

If you were to relax and begin to imagine the smells, textures and tastes of eating a juicy T-bone steak with roast potatoes (or whatever your favourite food is), you might end up hungry, and even begin to salivate at the

THE FIVE-MINUTE FEAR FIX

- *Click the thumb and forefinger on your non-writing hand and stimulate the neuro-vascular pressure points on your forehead.*
- *Review the memory to be dismantled.*
- *Contemplate the memory in black and white.*
- *Contemplate the black and white memory with no volume.*
- *Mentally distance yourself from the memory so that it feels smaller.*
- *Smile.*
- *Review the memory, changing negative aspects to extremely positive ones.*
- *Contemplate the memory with vibrant colours and perfect imagery added.*
- *Continue to contemplate the memory with its perfect sights and perfect sounds.*
- *Develop your mental appetite for success by feeling how wonderful it is to have succeeded beyond your wildest dreams!*

thought. If a short time later you passed a restaurant or visited the butcher, you might even act to overcome your hunger! If you have never experienced the delights of a T-bone with roast potatoes (or perhaps the only one you've eaten was burnt to a crisp), you won't become hungry at the thought of experiencing the food.

In the same way, by imagining the feeling of having succeeded, you develop a mental appetite that will help you achieve your goals. The most powerful and recent memories that will spontaneously occur to you from now on will be your mental successes. To summarise the method, the steps are set out in the box on the previous page.

Finally, before you move to the next chapter, I suggest you perform the Five-minute Fear Fix at least twice more in those areas of learning and memory in which you most want to experience success.

A BRAIN OWNER'S GUIDE

Have you ever wanted to unlock the brainpower you once had, to regain the sort of learning abilities that you had as a young child? Some theorists say we learn more during the first five years of life than we do in the next fifty, as we progressively use less of our 'three thinking brains'.

To find out where your 'three thinking brains' are, place your forefingers under each ear lobe. The part of your brain between your fingers is the non-thinking, autopilot brain stem, which is responsible for basic life supports, such as breathing. Now place your fingers on top of your ears. This part, the first of your 'three thinking brains', is the limbic system, which is responsible for emotions and survival behaviours, such a fighting, fleeing, feeding and sexual reproduction.

If you now place your forefingers on top of your head (like antennas) you will locate the left and right

  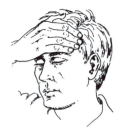

hemispheres of your neocortex, the second and third of your 'three thinking brains'. While both hemispheres are in constant communication, for most people the left hemisphere is responsible for language, analysing, counting, reading, writing, talking, thinking one thought at a time and controlling the right side of the body. The right hemisphere is non-verbal (intuitive), visual, creative, spatial, musical, thinks several thoughts simultaneously and operates the left side of the body. (Left-handed people often have a less clear-cut division between function of the right and left hemispheres. The procedures described in this book, however, cater for both right-handed and left-handed people.)

As young children, we were fascinated and excited by learning and, as a result, we used more of our limbic system in the learning process than adults do. (It's easy to remember what you enjoy and are emotionally involved with.) We were also much more imaginative, musical, curious, and visual – all right-brain functions. While adults tend to contemplate life via symbols such as numbers and letters, young children contemplate 'reality'. If I initially mention 'four' or 'cat' to my adult students, they usually process it as '4' or 'four' and the word 'cat'. A young child would think of ': :' and an image of a cat. As our memories are predominantly visual, it's natural that 60 per cent of young children have memories that are almost eidetic, or photographic. Unfortunately, through lack of stimulation, only about 10 per cent of adults have a similar memory capability.

Most young children learn rapidly, with a sense of excitement and whole-brain stimulation. The early school years are facilitated by art, rhymes, music and picture books. Then there is an ever-increasing emphasis on teaching the left-brain skills of reading, 'riting, 'rithmetic and analytical thinking. As the right brain becomes increasingly dormant, often the only time we engage in right-brain thinking is when we are distracted by 'inner music' and daydreams.

At night, when we are freer from analytical tasks, the

right brain becomes dominant and we experience hours of creative visual thinking. Upon waking, our bossy, verbal left brain takes over and shuts down our right brain, and we forget our dreams and lose our ability to generate visual imagery and have flashes of inspiration.

Interestingly, 95 per cent of scientific breakthroughs occur when people have access to their creative right-brain thinking. Einstein, for example, trusted his imagination and applied it to every discovery he made. After freeing his right brain to daydream, he would then use the maths of his left brain to prove true the theories he had 'imagined' when relaxed. You may be familiar with other examples of scientists using their right brains to make connections: Newton 'discovering' gravity while sitting under a tree with his apple, or Archimedes jumping out of his bathtub yelling 'Eureka!', having solved another complex problem.

Left Hemisphere:	*Right Hemisphere:*
language	images
logic	music
numbers	rhythm
analysis	imagination
reading	creativity
writing	colour
'four/4'	: :

No doubt you've occasionally been brilliant while dozing or under the shower, only to lose that inspirational thought as your judgmental left brain reasserted itself. Quite soon, I suspect you will have the confidence to go with your gut feelings, or right-brain thinking.

ENERGY EXERCISES

An unusual yet effective way to enhance your thinking ability is to use the following two 'energy exercises'. How do they work? Think of acupuncture or acupressure, forms of therapy that involve stimulating energy paths, or meridians, in your body.

Ten years ago, while eating at a restaurant in Hong Kong, I witnessed my first demonstration of acupressure. One of the people at the table was an Englishman named Stanley. He had been in a car accident a few weeks before and couldn't move his head from side to side without a great deal of pain. This was despite his taking anti-inflammatory drugs, visiting physiotherapists and seeing numerous doctors. It just so happened that a Dr Chan (who, I later found out, was in charge of one of the hospitals in Hong Kong) overheard Stanley's problem and offered to help.

The two went off to the side of the restaurant where Dr Chan started to press firmly on Stanley's lower back. For the next minute, Stanley's face went as red as a beetroot and any moment I thought he would scream out in pain. Then an amazing thing happened. As Stanley walked back to the table he began to move his head with ease!

When I asked Dr Chan what he had done, he said that the pain was associated with an energy blockage in the body. All that had to be done was release the energy in one particular meridian so that Stanley would release on the spot all the pain rather than block and accumulate it.

The two energy meridians of use to you are known as the receptive (conception) meridian, and the expressive (governing) meridian. By stimulating these energy pathways, you can alter your mental state according to your needs.

When you need to ponder, reflect upon or absorb information, stimulate your receptive energy meridian. To do this, place one hand on your pubic bone and the fingertips of your other hand on the centre of the cleft on your chin, just below your lower lip. For 30–60 seconds, breathe in through your nose and out through your mouth. With every breath you inhale, do your best to contemplate a white light flowing up the front of your body.

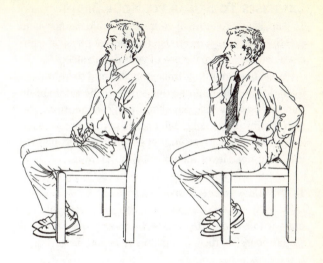

Stimulating the receptive meridian   Stimulating the expressive meridian

To be better able to 'think on your feet' and retrieve information, you can stimulate your expressive energy meridian. For this, touch your tail-bone with one hand and between your nose and upper lip with your other hand. Breathe as before (in nose, out mouth) and this time contemplate the stream of white light flowing up your spine.

EXERCISES TO STIMULATE YOUR BRAIN

To gain access to more of your whole-brain memory and creative powers, you can use two simple physical exercises and begin to make use of your dream sleep.

As we tend to be left-brained by day and right-brained by night, we can improve our ability to be whole-brain thinkers by activating our right brain each morning and our left brain each night. Before each of the physical exercises that follow, move your eyes in a sideways figure 8 with your head level and pointing to the front.

To stimulate your left brain

Each night just before going to sleep, kick-start your left brain with a two-part exercise. It relaxes your body and directs energy to the left hemisphere of your brain.

1. Place your left ankle on your right knee.
2. Put the palm of your right hand over the top of your left foot (where your shoelaces would be).
3. Thread your left hand under your right arm so that the fingers of both hands touch.

4 With closed eyes, breathe gently in through your nose and out through your mouth for 30–60 seconds.

Then go through these steps.

1 Rest the heels of your hands on your lap.
2 Join your fingertips together in an arch.
3 Rest the tip of your tongue on the roof of your mouth.
4 With closed eyes, breathe gently in through your nose and out through your mouth for 30–60 seconds.

After activating your left brain, say aloud, as if you really mean it, 'Tonight I remember my dreams!', and then expect soon to be able to wake up directly from a dream.

Each morning as soon as you are aware that you are waking, jot down one or two key words from a dream. (If possible avoid turning on any lights.) Keep a pen and pad next to your bed. Within ten to thirteen days you should be able to access your right brain and recall two or more dreams each morning.

To stimulate your right brain

After you've woken up, to prevent yourself reverting to left-brain dominance, cross-march for one minute, moving your right arm across your body to touch your left knee, and vice versa. Have your head level and pointing to the front and glance gently up to the left and back to the front, up to the left and back to the front . . .

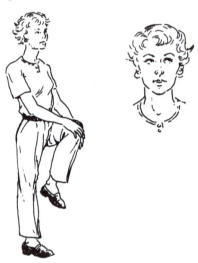

These exercises can be done any time you choose, depending on the type of thinking you need to do. For example, to remember a melody or enhance creativity and become a 'lateral thinker', you will benefit by cross-marching for at least 30 seconds before starting the task. To remember more technical information, and improve your concentration and analytical thinking abilities, do the two-part sitting exercise.

By using simple techniques such as these you will soon be able to:

- access the appropriate hemisphere of your brain for each type of thinking
- rediscover an excitement for learning
- become more intuitive
- improve your memory as you more effectively tap the potential of your 'three thinking brains'.

4
THE BRAIN CHAIN

In the first chapter you were required to remember a simple list of information. If you didn't do too well, it may have been because you only used half your brain. All the steps of reading, writing, talking and rote repetition mainly involve the left hemisphere of your brain. Think back to how easy or difficult those tests were.

Perhaps after recalling one item, you had to struggle just as hard to remember the next. In this chapter you will discover how to use your brain to lock in information, so the first thing you recall will trigger all the information you need – forwards or backwards! Then you will gain some insights into how you can benefit by applying these ideas to recalling your daily goals, or even to remembering a speech.

Before we begin, I'd like you to complete the questionnaire on the following pages. Tick your appropriate response.

QUESTIONNAIRE

Imagine that I've just returned from a holiday in China, and invited you over to my place for dinner. Would you rather watch a slide show of my holiday or the movie I've made from the video I took?

Slides ☐   *Movie* ☐

If you had had a holiday in Queensland, would it be easier for you to remember seeing a pineapple exaggerated out of all proportion, so that it was as big as a house, or a more normal-sized pineapple?

Realistic ☐   *Exaggerated* ☐

What do you think would be easier to remember: a picture of a male politician wearing a three-piece suit or the same politician wearing an absurd purple bikini?

Everyday suit ☐   *Absurd purple bikini* ☐

Do you think it would be quicker for a child to put away a toy train and numerous carriages if the carriages were linked together or separated?

Linked ☐ *Separated* ☐

Do you think that, if you were feeling relaxed, you would be reminded of something if you:

- *were at the beach and heard the distant musical bells of an ice-cream van?* Yes/No
- *tasted one of your favourite foods that you hadn't had for years?* Yes/No
- *sniffed a medicine that you hated taking as a child?* Yes/No
- *went to a park and kicked or threw a ball around?* Yes/No
- *saw an old school photo?* Yes/No

If you answered yes to any of the above, tick 'Sensory'. If you didn't answer yes to any of the above tick 'Non-sensory'.

Sensory ☐ *Non-sensory* ☐

If you're like most people, your answers would have been M, E, A, L, S.

Something visually striking is easier to recall. Quite often you may not notice something – for example, an animal – until it moves. Tourism operators will often exaggerate the significance of a landmark to create a memorable experience for tourists. Also, if you see something totally absurd you remember it – and most likely tell your friends!

Information that can be linked with something you already know will also be easier to remember. For example, you may know that both television and the Olympic games came to Australia in 1956, perhaps because they are linked in your memory because your first television experience was watching the Olympic Games.

THE MEALS METHOD

Have you ever wanted to get five or six household chores done? What if you decided that tomorrow you wanted to clean the fish tank, buy some lipstick as a present for your mother, pick up some doughnuts for your kids – who have also made you promise to take them to a wildlife reserve so that they can write a story about platypuses for school – and do the vacuuming? If this were your schedule, you could write each task on a noticeboard or in your diary, but even if you did this it would still be remarkably easy to miss out something important. You probably can't consult a noticeboard or carry a diary with you all the time, so you need a method that will help you remember your list of tasks.

So that enough energy is involved in your thinking process to ensure that goals become longer-term (neurochemical) memories rather than short-term (neuro-electrical) memories, I suggest you use the MEALS method to put information in sequence.

In a few moments you will visualise the list of tasks given above as a mental **M**ovie picture. It will also be an **E**xaggerated and **A**bsurd process in which each piece of information is **L**inked with another thought, and, as the world's greatest movie producer, you will also have **S**ensurround. This generates vivid colours, smells, tastes and fantastic sounds.

I'll give you some help to start off with, but right now I'd like you to click your thumb and index finger of your non-writing hand together, and leave the finger and thumb together. (In fact whenever you need to concentrate more effectively you will benefit from using this simple psychological trigger.) Next, activate your right brain with the cross-marching exercise described on page 34 and then stimulate your receptive energy meridian as explained on page 30.

Now, here are the steps for putting the information in sequence.

1. Look upwards, shut your eyes and picture a fish tank filled with swimming lipsticks. Do this for a few moments until you are aware of colours and movement.
2. Dismiss this thought from your mind. The next step is to picture in your mind those lipsticks squirting jam and poking holes in doughnuts.
3. Leave the previous thought aside and imagine the peculiar sight of those doughnuts being eaten by a giant platypus.
4. Perhaps the platypus is house-proud, so visualise the same platypus using a vacuum cleaner. Ask yourself once again to contemplate colours and movement in this absurd scene.
5. Visualise the vacuum cleaner cleaning the inside of the fish tank that you first thought of.

Each key idea that you have just locked into your longer-term memory will ensure that you can remember to get everything done. Instead of needing to write down your daily goals, you will be able simply to select a key thought that will remind you of what it is you want to achieve. For example, to remember what you want to clean, all you have to do is contemplate an image of your fish tank or whatever is an appropriate image for your situation. (Maybe your fish tank has been smelling a bit off for a while and has a few floating fish in it?) When you recall that image, you won't say 'Why did I picture a fish tank (or whatever)?', because you have selected an appropriate image that instantly reminds you to clean the fish tank. Just as if you had been to the local theatre and seen this on the silver screen, you will then remember that there were lipsticks splashing about in the fish tank. 'Aha! That reminds me to buy some lipstick!', you will think.

Take a few moments to close your eyes and do your best to complete your mental movie.

How did you go? Perhaps you found yourself thinking: 'The **lipsticks** jumped on some **doughnuts**, which were eaten by a huge **platypus**, which in turn used a **vacuum cleaner**, which ended up in the **fish tank**!' If you ended up with the fish tank, congratulations. If you experienced a mental block (or your mind went blank) all you have to do is sneak up on the missing key thought from behind.

To find out how this can easily be done, close your eyes and let the first visual image that pops into your mind trigger the preceding thought. Run the movie in reverse. Do this now.

While you may have found that took a little more concentration than before, I suspect that you probably did quite well. By starting and finishing with the same thought, you have changed the memory process from one of rote learning to one of using a whole-brain **brain chain**. It doesn't matter what you first remember, all the items are firmly linked together.

To remember the processes you follow when forming a brain chain, think of MEALS: Movement, Exaggeration, Absurdity, Linked ideas, and multi-Sensory thoughts. Obviously, the more senses and emotions you invoke in a brain chain, the more you use your limbic system, and the more likely it is that you will remember the key ideas.

A Russian journalist called Solomon Shereshevskii, who remembered everything in his life, is an example of just how powerful the brain chain is. As a child he accidentally stumbled across what I have called the MEALS technique, and very quickly it became a natural part of his thinking process. Russia's leading memory expert, Alexandr Luria, quizzed and tested Shereshevskii for thirty years and couldn't fault his memory. Even if he was asked questions such as, 'What information did I test you on, twenty years ago today?', Shereshevskii would not only get everything correct, he would also remember people's moods, the weather and even the clothes they wore! If given a list of things to remember, very quickly he could remember the items in forward or reverse order. Through using the MEALS technique, he had developed extraordinary powers of multi-sensory perception (MSP as opposed to ESP).

By the way, how's your memory holding up? Have a go at recalling the list of items that started with **fish tank**.

How did you go? Until you're familiar with the technique, I suggest you undertake a quick mental review within 4 minutes of creating a brain chain. With practice you will become faster and will be able to absorb the information with less effort. Also, I advise you to place the emphasis on speed, rather than on accuracy. The longer you take, the more likely it is that you will revert to being left-brain dominant. When practising memorising the lists that follow, aim to get faster and faster, filling in any gaps you have by making a quick review of the brain chains involved.

Do your best to convert the following lists to mental brain chains. You will find these brain chains useful when you come to Chapter 6. I have provided some suggestions for how the items in the list might be connected, to help you to begin memorising the items.

hen .... (bathing in a) .... tub
tub .... (smashed by giant) .... tooth

tooth	(crashes onto)	teapot
teapot	(heated by)	torch
torch	(smothered by)	tie
tie	(frazzled, becomes)	tinsel
tinsel	(wrapped around a)	tent
tent	(?)	tape recorder
tape recorder	(?)	towel
towel	(?)	hen

Now recall the ten lines one by one, checking and reinforcing the brain chain as you progress down the page. If you feel you may be remembering the sentences rather than the 'movie', try humming a tune as you go!

Treat the following lists in the same way, using the MEALS method to establish connections between items and to develop a brain chain. Pause for a few minutes between each list, then do your best, with your eyes closed, to recall it. Please note that the lists will be referred to again, so do your best to lock them into your longer-term memory.

trophy	truck
truck	troops
troops	tree
tree	trawler
trawler	tricycle

tricycle	trickster
trickster	trench
trench	train
train	trout
trout	trophy
throat	thumb
thumb	Thoo (an imaginary character)
Thoo	theatre
theatre	thorns
thorns	thigh
thigh	thimble
thimble	therapist
therapist	they (danced)
they (danced)	thousand
thousand	throat
phone	funnel
funnel	food
food	feet
feet	fork
fork	fireplace
fireplace	fiddle
fiddle	feather
feather	fete

fete	fountain
fountain	phone
hose	hut
hut	hoop
hoop	heater
heater	horse
horse	highway
highway	hippopotamus
hippopotamus	hell
hell	hay
hay	hound
hound	hose
soap	sun
sun	soup
soup	sea
sea	sauce
sauce	sign
sign	sick
sick	senate
senate	sail
sail	sow
sow	soap
vote	vulture
vulture	voodoo

voodoo ....veal
veal ....vault
vault ....vice
vice ....video
video ....vet
vet ....veil
veil ....voucher
voucher ....vote

goat ....gumboot
gumboot ....guru
guru ....geese
geese ....gauntlet
gauntlet ....guide
guide ....guitar
guitar ....ghetto
ghetto ....gate
gate ....gown
gown ....goat

nose ....nut
nut ....noose
noose ....knee
knee ....north
north ....knight
knight ....knit

knit	net
net	nail
nail	noun
noun	nose

Each night use the brain-chain method to programme tomorrow's tasks. Review the brain chain upon waking, and briefly visualise yourself getting things done and achieving those goals.

REMEMBERING SPEECHES AND ESSAYS

'Me? Make a speech? You've got to be joking. I'd rather die!'

How often have you heard, or perhaps even made, a statement like that? Does your throat seize up and your heart start racing at the mere thought of speaking in front of a group of people?

If it does, you are not alone. According to the *Book of Lists*, many people fear speaking in public more than death! Yet it's usually not a fear of speaking itself; rather, it's a fear that **forgetting** will lead to humiliation, ridicule and riotous laughter!

Perhaps the most boring speeches are those that are read out word for word. At the end of a speech I recently attended, the speaker gave out transcripts. They should have been given out first, so that I could have decided whether to remain and listen, or read it later. By reading his speech he also missed the vital body language of people fidgeting and looking at their watches, and, while the speech imparted a few gems, he went on for too long.

It's important to realise that you are communicating thoughts and ideas to your audience, not just words, so the golden rules of giving a speech are: never, never read it; and the shorter the better. A speech or talk lasting 35 minutes is also much easier for both you and your audience to remember than one lasting an hour.

The brain-chain two-step
The first step in remembering a speech (or indeed anything you may have to write) is to extract and memorise the key ideas you need to share with your audience. A good speech may only have six to nine key points, which are usually best communicated through the use of stories and examples. (The rules from the book *How to Win Friends and Influence People* can be listed on one and a half pages. The other 200 pages are stories and examples.) To extract the key points, look at the outline you've prepared, and note the headings or sub-headings contained in it.

Let's assume you are to give a pep talk to a national sales team about how they can become more productive. A skeletal outline could be as follows.

1. If you were to set your alarm **clock** 35 minutes earlier – and assuming four weeks' annual holiday – you could earn an extra 3.5 weeks' income each year.
2. While flying on a **plane** or driving long distances, you could have good reading material or cassettes to better yourself continually and make more productive use of travel time.
3. Another vital aspect of productivity is to set in order or priority 5 **goals** that you want to realise that day, and stick with them until they are done.
4. Better use of time can also be made if you avoid **queues**, such as heavy freeway traffic, the lunchtime crush in a cafeteria, or annoying bank queues. A slightly unusual time schedule will often work wonders.
5. It also makes sense to delegate some time-consuming activities to someone else. This might entail hiring a **secretary** who can do particular jobs more quickly than you.
6. More time could be invested on the **telephone**, to generate more business leads, provide customer service, save time and reduce travel costs.

You will probably agree with me that if you did your research and could remember the key ideas in bold from the outline above, it would be quite straightforward to remember an entire speech or essay on the subject of personal productivity.

The next step is to form a brain chain with these key ideas, so they just seem to pop into your mind as needed during the speech, or as you put pen to paper. The first key idea that then occurs to you will be all that is needed to remember the entire speech or essay, forwards or backwards.

1. Picture, with your eyes closed, an alarm **clock** sprouting wings and turning into a **plane** flying through the air. (It will help if you look up to your right visual field and close your eyes to visualise this.)
2. Now leave that thought aside, and contemplate that **plane** crashing into some **goal**posts. Deliberately involve multi-sensory thoughts of sights, sounds and feelings to lock this sequence into your memory. Do this quickly.
3. Were the goalposts from football or soccer? Next have the **goal**posts at the heads of two **queues** of impatient, pushing people. Check that you are concentrating enough to know how many angry people there are in the queues. Close your eyes for a moment.
4. Let those **queues** form the arms and legs of a giant **secretary** that you employ. Are you aware of any colours?

5 Form the thought of that **secretary** beginning to pull apart a **telephone**. Was the phone push button or rotary dial, and what colour was it?
6 Finally have the **telephone** smashing onto the alarm **clock** that you first thought of.

Quickly review the previous thought sequence, using the MEALS technique, and do your best to ensure that your ideas are full of action, exaggerated and absurd.

Now you've formed a circular brain chain in which any thought that first occurs to you will remind you of all the other key ideas in the sequence, forwards or backwards. If, for example, the first idea you think of is, 'Set five goals each day in order of priority', the thought of goals leads to queues, secretary, telephone, clock, plane and back to goals.

The longer or more detailed the speech or essay, the more key ideas you would use in the brain chain. (Using some of the ideas in Chapter 8 will ensure you remember complex facts and figures such as sales revenues and profits.)

As a check, make sure you can go backwards through the brain chain as well as forwards. Then if your mind ever goes blank when you are speaking or writing, simply pause by taking a sip of water or click the thumb and finger on your non-writing hand and review the brain chain, either forwards or backwards, until the next part of your topic pops into your mind. If you are giving a speech, your audience will simply think you are making a dramatic pause.

So the next time you are given the opportunity to make a speech, or have to remember a lengthy sequence of ideas, use the brain-chain technique and you will remember your information with ease and greatly impress your audience!

LEARNING LANGUAGE

Use the MEALS technique (Movement, Exaggeration, Absurdity, Linking ideas, multi-Sensory thoughts) to lock in the following images. (Sentences are given in groups for ease of memorisation; they are not sequential.) Really go overboard and enjoy yourself!

- Put some sticky black **tar** in a burning **lamp**.
- Place a **fur on your** bed's **pillow**.
- A little boy cuts his finger on a **knife** and wants to **kiss you**.

Review and reinforce the above ideas before you continue.

- Drink **vinegar** from a bottle, become **sick** and throw up.
- A **cow** fills your cup with **coffee**.
- A piece of roast **chicken** pops out of a **cuckoo** clock.

Review and reinforce the above ideas before you continue.

- Throw **coconuts** at some goose-stepping **Nazi** soldiers.
- A man has bulging yellow eyes. He says, '**My eye** is **eggs**'.
- **Smack** a naughty **fish**.

Review and reinforce the above ideas before you continue.

- Some **meat** sprouts **knees and arms**.
- Say '**Me chilly!**' and eat some piping-hot **rice**.
- Put a **Maggi** brand stock cube in a glass of **water**.

Review and reinforce the above ideas before you lock in the final two thoughts.

- Splash your hand in a tub of **butter** that feels **soggy**.
- Bop a man over the head with a huge **banana**; now the **man's dizzy**.

Quickly review these last two.

The Brain Chain

SWAHILI VOCABULARY

Swahili	Connecting thoughts	English
taa	You put sticky black tar in a . . .	lamp
feronya	There's fur on your . . .	pillow
kisu	The child who wants to kiss you has . . .	knife
siki	You're sick and throw up because . . .	vinegar
kahawa	A cow fills your cup with . . .	coffee
kuku	What pops out of the cuckoo clock?	chicken
Nazi	What happens to the goose-stepping Nazis?	coconuts
mayai	'My eye is . . .'	eggs
samaki	You smacked a . . .	fish
nyami	What sprouted knees and arms?	meat
mchele	'Me chilly' so I eat . . .	rice
maji	You put a Maggi stock cube in a glass of . . .	water
siagi	What felt soggy?	butter
man dizzy	What bopped him on the head?	banana

You were actually beginning to learn the Swahili language. By using the MEALS technique, just about any word can be quickly and easily mastered. As you may already have a snippet of French, German or Indonesian, I've chosen a more unusual-sounding language for you.

Before I explain exactly why you did what you did, do your best to match the correct English word with each Swahili word in the list on the previous page. Cover the right hand column first. The words in the middle are to help you retrieve the correct meaning. Good luck!

You've probably done very well, so congratulations!

Conventional language tapes, while important for mastering an accent, are a much slower means of building vocabulary. Indeed if you had used conventional language tapes, it could have taken you up to two hours to lock those words into your longer-term memory. Perhaps you learnt most of them in a matter of minutes? Any English word that is unfamiliar to you can also be mastered in this way, as I hope to prove in a moment.

Applying the MEALS method to English

The key to developing an interest in learning new information is to become curious, treat all learning as a mind game, and imagine that you are already an expert. To convert a word into something that can be visualised, say the word slowly or quickly, or even slightly differently. This will then begin to generate a spark of creativity from your right hemisphere.

To demonstrate with English words, I've just opened my dictionary at random, and selected the word 'fugleman', meaning 'soldier placed in front of regiment while drilling to show the motions and time'. If you were to say the word slowly, it could sound like 'phew, girl, man'. Visualise marching soldiers chanting 'Phew, it's good we've got a girl, man, to show us how to drill!' This doesn't make much sense, yet you'll find the word fugleman more memorable now. If a word is intangible and can't be easily visualised – for example 'love' – substitute another image, such as two people kissing.

I've chosen another random word, 'hoggin', a word meaning a mixture of sand and gravel. This time it's very simple to remember the word – visualise a pig (hog) rolling in the sand and gravel. You should be getting the idea. With practice, you can begin to think creatively and visually much more rapidly than you can think logically.

Once you are familiar with the brain chain, it will be time for you to master the skill of remembering names and faces.

5

NAMES AND FACES

(Oh no, I don't believe it! Has he seen me yet? Aarghh – here he comes!)

'Hello Robin! Fancy meeting you here. It's great to see you again. I had a meeting with my finance manager and he's given me the go-ahead to talk about swinging some business your way.'

(How could I forget his name? After all that work . . .)

'Great! I'll get onto it right away, but tell me, what was your name again?'

Have you ever felt embarrassed and 'lower than a sleeping ant' because you had to ask for someone's name, possibly only minutes after having heard it?

By the time you finish reading this sentence, 714 683 names will have been forgotten around the world! Potential friends are being insulted and lucrative business opportunities lost right now.

Does your memory for names work like magic – by

disappearing? People attending memory-training seminars have gained a great deal of confidence and self-esteem by learning how to lock names and faces into their memory. Now it's your turn.

So often people say they never forget a face, yet are hopeless at putting a name to the face. When we meet people we usually look at their faces for some time, so it's relatively easy to remember a face. Names, however, are usually dealt with in about three seconds and tend to go in one ear and out the other. Has anyone ever come up to you and said, 'I remember your name, but I can't think of your face'? I doubt it.

Very often the problem is 'not getting' the name rather than 'forgetting'. You are either thinking about whether your hair is neat, your tie straight and your teeth clean *or* the name of the person you are meeting. If your mind is somewhere else at the time of an introduction, that's where the name will end up – somewhere else!

THE TECHNIQUES

The first and fairly obvious thing to do is to make sure you actually hear people's names. If they mumble or there's a background noise, say 'I'm sorry, I didn't get your name clearly'. They will be pleased that you care enough to make an effort. If you smile, and offer your name first, the person you are meeting will be more likely to respond clearly. Then use the person's name and ask a meaningful question that can't be answered with a yes or a no. This process of repeating a name after first hearing it will increase the likelihood of your recalling it by about 30 per cent.

While the other person is replying to your question, tilt your head slightly, glance up to the left and mentally project the name onto the speaker's forehead. With a blink of your eyes, take a mental photo. This method of focusing on a name is surprisingly effective and easier than it sounds. Unless the other person is taller than you, it will be necessary to lower your chin slightly while gently tilting your head so that you can move your eyes up to your left as you 'project' the name.

To reinforce this technique for putting a name to a face use the following method, which will allow you to remember the name itself and to recall it when you come face to face with its owner. First take notice of any prominent feature that makes the face of the person in question appear unique to you. This feature could be a scar, smile lines, a big nose, sunspots, thick lips, narrow eyes, a double chin, bushy eyebrows, a wrinkled forehead, or indeed anything that is likely to be noticed again when you next meet. For this reason avoid choosing hairstyle, jewellery or clothing, as these may well be different when you next meet.

After you've observed the face and chosen a facial feature, substitute a picture (a 'nameture') for the person's name and then mentally connect the nameture in an inventive way with the feature you've chosen.

Let's assume you've just met Ernest whose feature is bushy eyebrows. If no nameture instantly occurs to you inwardly reinforce the name either quickly or slowly. 'Ernest' said slowly may trigger the nameture 'urn' or, when you say it quickly, you may come up with 'a nest'. The next step is to combine the nameture with the bushy eyebrows. This simply requires a thought that an urn is being emptied on the eyebrows or the bushy eyebrows are a nest. To begin with I suggest you say to yourself, 'Ernest's eyebrows are a nest', and, when you feel comfortable with the technique, visualise a nest over his eyes instead of eyebrows.

The next time you see that face and those eyebrows an urn or a nest will come to mind and common sense will remind you of Ernest. While he may be delighted that you've remembered him, it's best not to tell him how you remembered his name. It's better to say you've just got a good head for names.

If you were to meet a Theresa and her feature was high cheekbones, you could mentally plant trees (Theresa) on those cheekbones so that when you saw them again you would be reminded of trees and the name

Theresa would pop into your mind. You can be confident that you won't say 'Hi, Trees!' because you know trees is not a name.

Exactly the same principles apply if a person volunteers his or her surname. The nameture for Isaacs could be 'eyes' or 'ice sacks' depending again on how quickly you said the name. There is no such thing as a poor nameture.

Now you have a technique that directs your attention to a name and connects it indelibly to a face. Even if you can't come up with a nameture, you've truly concentrated and will remember the name anyway.

You can't lose!

SOCIAL OCCASIONS

Use a person's name in conversation but don't overdo it. The use of a name is like a compliment, and nothing spoils a compliment like over-use. Start off with the name when you ask the initial question, use it once or twice during the conversation, and then again when saying goodbye.

When meeting several people, don't let yourself be rushed by an eager host. Take your time to master the names of everyone you have a conversation with, and quickly review the names after every third person. Arriving early at a meeting or social gathering also helps because you can learn names one by one as the guests arrive.

A useful tip to remember when starting to use these techniques is to jot down the names of the people you've met that day, and later review how you've remembered their names.

NAMETURES

To help you become more familiar with the ideas in this chapter, 200 nametures follow. Read over the list and then return to the beginning. Cover up my suggestions and do your best to come up with some of your own. This is also a great exercise to develop your creative right-brain thinking.

NAME-PICTURE SUBSTITUTES (NAMETURES)
Female

ABBY	a bee	ANNIE	a knee
ABIGAIL	a big ale	AUDREY	a tree
ADRIENNE	a drain	BARBARA	barber
AGNES	egg nest	BEATRICE	beat rice
ALICE	lice	BECKY	bicky
AMANDA	a man	BERYL	bear ill
ANASTASIA	ants stay here	BRENDA	blender
ANGELA	angel	CAMILLA	camel
ANITA	anteater	CARMEL	caramel
ANNE	ant	CINDY	cinder
ANNABEL	a new bell	CLAUDETTE	clawed at
ANNETTE	a net	COLLEEN	clean

Names and Faces

CRYSTAL	crystal	HOLLY	holly
CYNTHIA	sin tear	HONEY	honey
DALE	day old	INGRID	ink red
DAPHNE	deaf knee	IRENE	green
DEBBIE	deb	IVY	ivy
DELILAH	li-lo	JANE	chain
DENISE	dentist	JESSICA	chase a car
DIANNE	dyin'	JILL	chill
DONNA	doona	JOYCE	juice
DOREEN	door in	JUDITH	chewed it
EILEEN	eye lean	JULIE	jewellery
ELIZABETH	lizard bath	KATE	cake
EMMA	hammer	KATHY	cat see
ERICA	a wrecker	KAY	key
EVELYN	a violin	LAVERNE	love urn
FLORENCE	floor	LILY	lily
GERMAINE	germ	LINDA	lint
GINA	china	LOLITA	lolly eater
GINGER	ginger	LOUISE	low ice
HEATHER	heather	LUCILLE	loose ear
HELEN	hailin'	LUCINDA	loose cinder

MABEL	my bell	PENNY	penny
MAGGIE	magpie	PHOEBE	frisbee
MARGE	match	RENEE	grenade
MARIA	marry her	ROBYN	bin
MARIE	mare	ROSA	rose
MARJORIE	margarine	SAMANTHA	saw man
MARSHA	marsh	SARAH	share her
MARTINA	martini	SHARON	shine
MEG	mug	SHERRY	sherry
MEREDITH	merry dish	SYLVIA	silver
MONICA	harmonica	SUE	sioux
NAN	nun	THERESA	trees
NICOLE	nickel	VICKY	V key
OLIVIA	a liver	VIOLET	violet
OPHELIA	orphan	WENDY	windy
PEG	peg	YVETTE	a vet

Male

ABE	ape	ALEX	legs
ABRAHAM	a broom	ALFRED	half red
ALAN	a lens	ANDREW	hand drew
ALASTAIR	a last hair	ANTHONY	ant honey

ARCHIE	archer	*DOUGLAS*	da glass
ARTHUR	author	*DUNCAN*	dunny can
BARRY	berry	*ELLERY*	celery
BEN	bent	*EMANUEL*	a man
BERT	bird	*ERNEST*	a nest
BILL	bill	*EVAN*	a van
BRAD	bread	*FRANK*	frankfurt
BRIAN	brain	*FRED*	fried
BRUCE	bruise	*GARY*	carry
CAMERON	camera	*GERALD*	chair old
CHARLES	charred	*GRANT*	granite
CHRIS	cross	*GREG*	grog
CHRIS-	kissed a	*HANS*	hands
TOPHER	fur	*HARRY*	hairy
CLIFF	cliff	*HENRY*	hen ray
COLIN	coal in	*HERBERT*	her boot
CRAIG	crack	*HUGH*	ewe
DARRYL	drill	*IAN*	iron
DAVID	dazed	*JACK*	jack
DENNIS	tennis	*JAMES*	'jarmies'
DONALD	'duck'	*JEFF*	chef

JIM	gym	PERRY	pear
JONATHAN	join a tin/ apple	PETE	peat
		PHILLIP	flip
JOSEPH	shows off	RALPH	rough
JULIAN	jewel in	RAY	ray
KEITH	keys	RICHARD	wreck shed
KEVIN	cave in	RICK	wreck
LARRY	lorry	ROBERT	robber
LEO	lion	RODNEY	rod knee
LEOPOLD	leap pole	RONNIE	runny
LOU	'loo'	ROSS	moss
LUCAS	low kiss	SAMUEL	a mule
MALCOLM	mail come	SEAN	shorn
MARK	mark	SIDNEY	sit knee
MATTHEW	mat ewe	SILVESTER	silver vest
MAURICE	more rice	SIMON	sigh man
MICHAEL	make ill	STAN	stand
NICHOLAS	nickels	STEVE	stove
NORMAN	no man	STU	stew
OLIVER	olive	TED	tired
PAUL	pail	THEODORE	see a door

TIM	time	*WALLACE*	walrus
TOM	tom toms	*WALTER*	water
TONY	toe knee	*WAYNE*	weighin'
TYRONE	throne	*WILBUR*	wool bear
VINNIE	vinegar	*ZACK*	sack

By reading over this list a few times and inventing your own nametures, you will become more familiar and confident with the technique. Obviously if you meet a Darryl and use the nameture drill, the next time you meet a Darryl use the same nameture. Soon you'll have nametures for most of the people you meet.

To remember both first and last names, link them together using the MEALS technique. For example: a gale blows the beetles off (Gail Beeton); he plays tennis with legs of lamb (Dennis Lamb); trees are planted with the ferns (Theresa Fernandez); the clock flips from side to side (Phillip Clark); a robin 'tweets' the saxophone (Robyn Saxton); he needs a strong arm to build a nest (Ernest Armstrong).

6

YOUR MENTAL FILING CABINET

Recently a friend walked up to a young child and politely asked her if she would like to learn how to count up to ten. Needless to say the answer was an emphatic NO! Toy cars were much more interesting than numbers.

Think back to the time when you were four or five years old. Were you thrilled the first time someone attempted to teach you the twenty-six letters of the alphabet? If you were, it was because you understood that there would be some kind of benefit; for example simply earning the praise of your parents.

You see, we invest time in learning when it has some kind of 'pay-off' or benefit for us. No doubt you now know, as an adult, how essential it was for you to invest your time and energy learning numbers or the letters of the alphabet.

Now that you're approximately half-way through this

book it's time to learn an extremely simple memory system that will help you for the rest of your life.

THE NUMBERS 1 TO 10

We know that most learning involves connecting two concepts, using the left side of the brain. To remember to visit a dentist at 1.00 pm, for example, would usually mean writing the number 1 next to the word 'dentist': both left-brain concepts. Perhaps you have heard the expression 'a picture is worth a thousand words'? Well, I firmly believe **a visualisation is worth a hundred repetitions**. Surely, if you witnessed a sticky cream bun being pushed into the face of a dentist, you would find that memorable. The reading, writing or repeating of 'dentist 1' is, on the other hand, exceedingly boring and quite forgettable.

To ensure that information passes through our left (verbal/numerical) hemisphere, right (creative/visual) hemisphere, and our limbic system or 'emotion brain', it's necessary to connect dentist and 1 in a visual and emotive way. While it's quite easy to visualise what a dentist looks like, numbers, being symbols, are a little more difficult to visualise. To make it easy we will simply use a rhyming substitute for the number one, and in this case we will use the word and image 'bun'.

Now do your best to use your multi-sensory perception to connect a bun with a dentist. Make sure that you use the ideas from the previous chapters and involve movement, absurdity and exaggeration. (You could, for example, mentally experience yourself pushing a cream bun into the face of a dentist.) Do this now.

How did you go? Again I suggest you mentally check that you are aware of colour and movement when forming these thoughts in your mind. This, you may have discovered, requires your full concentration, so before we continue it's a good idea to have a good yawn, stretch and perhaps even have a glass of water.

The exercise you just did used one of the appointments from the list in the appointments test in Chapter 1. Let's take the other appointments from this list and lock them into your longer-term memory using a set of number pictures. (From now on these will be called 'numtures'.)

1 Quickly review your picture of yourself pushing a cream bun into the face of a dentist.
2 At 2.00 pm you need to make an important phone call, so you can lock this into your memory (for as long as you need to) by mentally experiencing yourself smashing your **shoes** on a rapidly disintegrating **tele-**

phone. What sort of phone did you smash? Was it push button or rotary dial, and what colour was it? If you're not sure I suggest you quickly review the scene and focus your concentration even more.

3 At 3.00 pm you need to remember to purchase a tub of butter, so contemplate a three-legged **skier** carrying a tub of **butter** as he or she is falling into yellow butter-like snow.

4 The 4.30 appointment is to pick up a hearing aid for a relative. Visualise a gigantic **hearing aid** smashing a **door** in half.

5 The next item on your schedule is to turn on an electric radiator at 5.30 pm. Picture a **radiator** taking a huge **dive** off a diving board. The radiator is so large that it snaps the diving board in half!

6 Your **tax return** is to be filled out at 6 o'clock, so picture yourself scratching the form with a bundle of old **sticks**.

7 At 7.00 am you are to catch a bus. Imagine you are catching a **bus** in your **seventh heaven** among the clouds.

8 At 8.15 am you want to remember to go on a bike ride, so visualise an **ape** covered in apple **cores** riding a **bicycle**.

9 Your task soon after is to buy a handbag (at 9.00 am). For this smash some bottles of **wine** over a **handbag**.

10 The cricket highlights are on television at 10.00 pm.
Visualise some **hens** playing **cricket**.

Once learnt, the ten numtures can be used over and over for different purposes whenever you need to lock one of these numbers into your memory.

To become more familiar with these numtures, I suggest you have a go at writing them down, describing them with one or two adjectives and then drawing them.

NUMTURES FOR 1 TO 10

NUMBER	NUMTURE	DESCRIPTION
1	bun	sticky cream bun
2	shoe	
3	ski	
4	door	
5	dive	
6	sticks	
7	seventh heaven	
8	ape	
9	wine	
10	hen	

Look for any connection that might help you learn the numtures more rapidly. For example, the door has four corners, the wine is 9 per cent alcohol, there are ten hens, you wear two shoes, and so on.

To know if the appointment is night or day is usually obvious, but in case you need to differentiate between the two, simply make the daytime appointments visually vivid and the evening or night-time images a little duller. To remember to do something on the half hour, all that is required is visually to chop the numture in half. Half a door means 4.30, and so on. Perhaps you also recalled an ape covered in apple cores riding a bicycle. Including exaggerated apple cores in your thoughts will remind you that the intended time is a 'coreter' past the hour. If you needed to lock in 9.45, you could connect your appointment with a bottle of wine being smashed by a .45-calibre handgun.

Jot down the numbers 1 to 10 and do your best to recall both the numtures and the connected appointments.

THE NUMBERS 11 TO 19

When we get up to the two-figure numbers in the tens, we use an effective system that has been in use for many years. The numtures all start with a 't', representing the ten, and then have a vowel sound that rhymes with that

NUMTURES FOR 11 TO 19

Number		First sound	First vowel sound	Numture	Description
11	10+1	t	u	tub	yellow enamel, has two taps that look like 'll'
12	10+2	t	oo	tooth	jagged edges, 12 m high, weighs 12 kg
13	10+3	t	ee	teapot	unlucky, spills tea
14	10+4	t	aw	torch	burning, smoky
15	10+5	t	eye	tie	red, half-price at sale, was $30
16	10+6	t	i	tinsel	red, green and yellow, for Christmas
17	10+7	t	e	tent	green canvas, at camp-site 17
18	10+8	t	ay	tape recorder	blue, playing a Rolling Stones song loudly
19	10+9	t	ow	towel	has a fringe and picture on it

of the digit of the number. This may sound complex, yet it's really quite straightforward and comes easily with practice. Again, I suggest you write them down with a description and then draw them.

You may have noticed that we are more interested in how the numbers sound than how they are spelled. If the number 1 was spelled according to the way it sounds, it would be 'wun'. Therefore to create a numture for the number 11, we have a 't' as we are in the tens, and a short 'u' sound as it's the rhyming vowel sound from the digit 1 in the units.

Where possible, create an unusual connection between the number and your numture. While you could work out that 'teapot' means 13, as it starts with a 't' (for tens) and the 'ea' rhymes with 'three', you will learn the numture more rapidly and more permanently if, for example, you make the teapot *unlucky*.

You could also work out that 12 means 'tooth', because the numture must start with a 't', as we're in the tens, and then rhyme with 'two': t + oo = tooth. If, however, you made the tooth yellow, full of cavities with jagged edges and *12 metres high*, you would lock the knowledge in more effectively!

You may have been a bit puzzled by the numture 'towel' for the number 19. As we have already used the 'eye' sound for the number 15 (to get 'tie') we have to use a different sound. The little story following is useful in helping you remember that the sound we use when we have a 9 to rhyme with in two-figure numbers is 'ow'.

Very few people actually know that the shape of the number 9 originated from a pair of scissors. One day an absent-minded scientist was working out what shape to use for the number 9. As he sat down he broke a pair of scissors that he had forgotten was in his back pocket. With a loud 'ow!!' he pulled out half the pair of scissors (9) and that's how the shape of the number 9 was created.

Mental pictures make information memorable

Do you know what shape Italy is? What about France? Pause for a moment and see if anything pops into your mind. While it's possible you never learnt these facts, if, many years ago, a teacher showed you and your friends in class how Italy looks like a woman's boot, it's likely you still remember this today. The information was memorable because it appealed to your right, visual/creative hemisphere and aroused a response (excitement) from your limbic system.

I'll give you another example of how you might stimulate whole-brain learning. Do you know which camel has two humps and which has one hump? (It will help if you abandon all analytical thinking and imagine that for the next minute or so you are six years of age.)

Well, one day a Dromedary fell down a large hole and all that was left visible was a **D** sideways. Then along came a Bactrian camel and it too fell down the hole until all that was visible was a **B** sideways. Pretty simple, isn't it, yet very effective! **B** for two humps, **D** for one hump.

Come to think of it, just about all learning during our early years at school is directed at our left *and* right brains. Nursery rhymes, songs, picture story books and even spelling rules such as 'i before e except after c' all force us to use our right brain. But as we progress through school we are instructed, 'Don't have such a vivid imagination!', even though wise people (such as Einstein, who broke the rules of conventional thinking as well as spelling) have claimed that imagination is more important than knowledge.

THE NUMBERS 20 TO 99

Now we arrive at the twenties, but we'll call them 'trenties' because there aren't enough rhyming words to start them with 'tw'. So, all our visual substitutes for numbers start with 'tr' and then rhyme with the vowel of the digit. For example, the numture for 23 will start with 'tr' as we're in the trenties and then rhyme with 'three' to give us 'tree'. Taking the number 25 we will have 'tr' for trenty and an 'eye' sound from 'five' to give us 'tricycle'. Again, when we get to 29 the vowel sound will be 'ow' and the resulting numture will be 'trout'. If you needed to remember that a wedding was held on the 29th you could lock the memory in by visualising two trout being married. It would then be a simple matter to ask yourself later on, 'What did I visualise for the 29th?', and a wedding would come to mind as you contemplated what you'd seen the trout getting up to. If you needed to remember the date of a wedding that you had to attend, all you would have to do is recall how you visualised the wedding and 'trout/29' would pop into your mind.

The chart on the following pages plus the numtures on pages 75 and 77 contain all the numtures you will need to know to be able to lock in 1000 bits of information should the need ever arise. As you read over the numtures, some of them may appear familiar to you.

Before I explain how you can learn these numtures quickly and easily, I'll tell you how we get each group of numbers. The first ten numtures simply rhyme with their numbers: 1 bun; 2 shoe; 3 ski; 4 door; 5 dive; 6 sticks; 7 seventh heaven; 8 ape; 9 wine; 10 hen. Then the numtures in the tens start with 't' and the twenties start with 'tr' (there aren't enough words to start them all with 'tw'), as already explained; the thirties start with 'th'; the forties

NUMTURES FOR 20 TO 99

Tr	Th	F	H	Vowel sounds
20 trophy	30 throat	40 phone	50 hose	oh
21 truck	31 thumb	41 funnel	51 hut	u
22 troops	32 Thoo	42 food	52 hoop	oo
23 tree	33 theatre	43 feet	53 heater	ee
24 trawler	34 thorns	44 fork	54 horse	aw
25 tricycle	35 thigh	45 fireplace	55 highway	eye
26 trickster	36 thimble	46 fiddle	56 hippo	i
27 trench	37 therapist	47 feather	57 hell	e
28 train	38 they	48 fete	58 hay	ay
29 trout	39 thousand	49 fountain	59 hound	ow

S	V	G	N	Vowel sounds
60 soap	70 vote	80 goat	90 nose	oh
61 sun	71 vulture	81 gumboot	91 nut	u
62 soup	72 voodoo	82 guru	92 noose	oo
63 sea	73 veal	83 geese	93 knee	ee
64 sauce	74 vault	84 gauntlet	94 north	aw
65 sign	75 vice	85 guide	95 knight	eye
66 sick	76 video	86 guitar	96 knit	i
67 enate	77 vet	87 ghetto	97 net	e
68 ail	78 veil	88 gate	98 nail	ay
69 sow	79 voucher	89 gown	99 noun	ow

start with 'f'; the fifties start with 'h' (as we've used 'f' for forties and we're **h**alf-way there); the sixties start with 's'; the seventies start with 'v' (we've just used 's' for the sixties and 'v' is the next consonant in 'seventies'); the eighties start with 'g' (the first consonant in 'eighties'); and the nineties start with 'n'. The vowel sounds of the numbers between 11 and 99 rhyme with those of the relevant digits, with the exception of the nines, as already explained. The additional vowel sound you will notice in the chart above – 'oh' – has been chosen as the vowel sound for 20, 30, 40, 50, 60, 70, 80 and 90 because 'o' is one name for the nought in all these numbers.

APPLYING THE BRAIN CHAIN TO NUMBERS

Right now you may be thinking, 'No way will I ever be able to learn so many numtures. It took me years to learn the alphabet and there were only twenty-six things to remember! And yet, if you have practised the brain-chain technique on the lists in Chapter 4, you've probably already learnt them. Each list of ten items on pages 44–9 in Chapter 4 represented ten numtures. Let's have a look at a couple of those practice lists and you'll see what I mean.

hen............	(bathing in a)................	tub	10 hen
tub	(smashed by giant).....	tooth	11 tub
tooth.........	(crashes onto).............	teapot	12 tooth

teapot ....(heated by) ....torch		13 teapot
torch ....(smothered by) ....tie		14 torch
tie ....(frazzled, becomes) ....tinsel		15 tie
tinsel.........(wrapped around a)....tent		16 tinsel
tent ....(?).................................tape recorder		17 tent
tape recorder ...(?)..............................towel		18 tape recorder
towel.........(?).................................hen		19 towel

trophy...truck	20 trophy
truck ....troops	21 truck
troops ....tree	22 troops
tree..trawler	23 tree
trawler..tricycle	24 trawler
tricycle ....trickster	25 tricycle
trickster..trench	26 trickster
trench ....train	27 trench
train ....trout	28 train
trout..trophy	29 trout

Until you've mastered the numtures you may find it helps to put them on a wall chart or to make a copy of them to keep in your handbag or wallet so that you can look over them while you're waiting for your bus.

Your Mental Filing Cabinet

PRACTISING WHOLE-BRAIN LEARNING

If at all possible I suggest you experience this section of the book with a friend. You will each take turns at communicating information and then absorbing information. If you can't practise this with a friend, relax, take your time and have fun anyway.

- The communicator stimulates the expressive energy meridian for approximately 20 seconds while the listener stimulates the receptive energy meridian, as detailed on pages 30–1.
- The listener's eyes are closed while the other person communicates the first of the following ideas in an energetic, enthusiastic way, emphasising the words in bold type. The listener contemplates the idea, with thumb and finger joined. Once aware of either some colour or movement in an idea, the listener nods and then absorbs the next idea.
- After five ideas have been conveyed, the communicator quizzes the listener, using half the idea; for example, 'What was the **ape** wearing?', 'What was taking a **dive**?' Reinforce any ideas not fully absorbed.
- Roles are swapped after the five ideas have been reviewed and the next five ideas are used. Switch roles until both people have absorbed all twenty ideas.

An **ape** wearing an **oxygen** mask.
A **bun** floating in the air like a **hydrogen** balloon.
Your **door** being opened by a **bear that's ill (yum!)**.
Eating the **heel (yum!)** on your **shoe**.
A wild **boar on** a diving board takes a **dive**.
A **knight rowin'** a boat up in **seventh heaven**.
Smashing **sticks** onto an old, burnt **car**.
A **skier** eating **liver (yum!)**.
A **neon** sign on a **hen**.
Getting some **furs for us** to match our **tie**.
Sneezing with the **flu** as you drink **wine**.
Noah's **ark on** a tape recorder.
Coloured **tinsel** wrapped around rotten eggs that **sell for** 16 cents.
Pouring the contents of an unlucky **teapot** onto an **aluminium** soft-drink can.
A **tub** full of bubbly **soda (yum!)**.
A **trophy** with milk from **cows (yum!)**.
A **silly comb** being warped by a burning **torch**.
A **tooth** weighing 12 kilograms **mangling knees**.
Potatoes (yum!) on a large beach **towel**.
A **tent** in a swimming **pool smelling of chlorine**.

How did you go? Please review those ideas that are not yet in your longer-term memory. I'll still be here when you get back, so feel free to take as much time as you need.

Believe it or not, what you were beginning to learn is widely regarded in schools as being the difficult information to remember: a chart of over 100 chemical elements. What makes chemistry difficult to remember is the fact that it is almost impossible to know what these different chemicals look like. Do you know what argon or potassium looks like? Probably not, so in order to visualise them, I suggest you use a substitute image that will remind you of the chemical.

The easiest way to arrive at a substitute is to say the word (with your eyes level) and simply use the first idea that occurs to you. Argon may become 'ark on' while potassium may become 'potatoes (yum!)'. The ark was on a tape recorder, so argon is number 18. The potatoes were on a towel, so that will soon trigger for you the fact that potassium is number 19 in that complex chart of chemicals.

On the following page you will discover a list of the first twenty chemical elements. Unfortunately they are all out of order and it's your job to use the numtures to work out the number for each chemical element. Taking the first one, what was the connected thought with 'furs for us'? I suggest you close your eyes and think back to what you did with the 'furs for us'. It's quite likely you were matching them with a tie: 't' (ten) and 'ie' (five) gives us

CHEMICAL ELEMENTS

Element	Nameture	Number	Numture (in order)
phosphorus	furs for us	15	1 bun
neon	neon sign	10	2 shoe
lithium	liver (yum!)		3 ski
carbon	burnt car		4 door
nitrogen	knight rowin'		5 dive
boron	boar on		6 sticks
helium	heel (yum!)		7 seventh heaven
beryllium	bear ill		8 ape
hydrogen	balloon		9 wine
oxygen	oxygen mask		10 hen
chlorine	swimming pool		11 tub
potassium	potatoes (yum!)		12 tooth
magnesium	mangled knees		13 teapot
silicon	silly comb		14 torch
calcium	cows (yum!) milk		15 tie
sodium	soda (yum!)		16 tinsel
aluminium	drink can		17 tent
sulphur	rotten eggs that sell for		18 tape recorder
argon	ark on		19 towel
fluorine	flu wine		20 trophy

Your Mental Filing Cabinet

15. Obviously, it's very difficult to know what neon looks like, so simply visualise a neon sign with your numture for 10 and you'll lock it in. The numtures are written down in order on the right-hand side, but mainly concern yourself with matching the two parts of your multi-sensory ideas and you'll learn the numbers with practice. Now I'll leave the rest up to you.

Obviously, if you had trouble recalling the numtures for some of the chemicals you could simply have scanned the right-hand side of the list until you found the correct numtures, but it's much better to be able to obtain them straight from your memory.

The uses of this system for memory are limitless. They could be: remembering the weather forecast, remembering a date of the month, remembering times, learning facts both in and out of order, and on and on . . .

Also, once you are familiar with your rhyming number pictures (numtures), whenever you read articles or listen to talks with such titles as 'Six steps to business success', or 'Eight easy ways to sell your service', you will be able to memorise what you hear as you hear it and what you read as you read it. Simply connect a key idea, in a visual way, with your numtures!

7

OVERCOMING ABSENT-MINDEDNESS

Did you know that Albert Einstein once forgot where he lived? He would have called home, but he had also forgotten his phone number! More recently a president of the United States forgot what country he was in. If such people can be absent-minded I'm sure that anyone can.

'Absent-mindedness' is simply that – your mind is absent when you need to pay attention. Even memory experts are known to be absent-minded every now and then. Whether you are paying attention is not determined by age; motivation is, however, a strong determining factor.

Do and think anything if it helps you remember!

THE TECHNIQUES

You overcome absent-mindedness by making yourself pay attention. The following methods may appear unusual, but, rest assured, with regular use you will find yourself much more aware and alert.

'Explode' objects

Look around you and choose a part of the room to look at. Now imagine that you have a pair of glasses in your hand and you start focusing light through those glasses in such a way that you begin to burn that part of the room. Take a second or two to do this.

That really made you pay attention! If you arrive home and place your glasses on the dining-room table and want to remember where you put them, for a split second imagine seeing that table set on fire by your glasses. Imagine the hot, crackling flame, the smoke rising upwards and the smell of the burning table. It might only take half a second, but you will know where you last put your glasses.

If you tend to forget where you put your keys, simply imagine they are a hand grenade and every time you put them down mentally explode the keys. If you put them on the top of the refrigerator imagine you've just blown a hole in it! Even if you exploded the television yesterday and the rocking chair the day before, you will discover you always remember the most recent explosion and that will be where you put your bunch of keys most recently.

Take mental photos

Another method to overcome absent-mindedness is as follows. As you place your wallet or purse on a kitchen bench, 'click-blink' your eyes and imagine you've just taken a mental photo with your eyes.

Adapt these ideas to remember other things you might forget, such as umbrellas, slippers, pens and books. After a while you will find yourself 'naturally' remembering where you put things.

Talk to yourself

Another way of making yourself aware of what you are doing is to use 'self-talk'. As you put a newspaper on a bookshelf, say to yourself, 'Paper on bookshelf'.

Have you ever wondered why you've just opened the pantry cupboard? To make sure you always know why, first focus your attention by saying to yourself, 'Get some biscuits' or whatever is relevant. You could even mentally preview opening the cupboard door only to have hundreds of biscuits fall onto the floor! Take that half-second and when you walk into the kitchen and open that door, you will be thinking biscuits!

Give yourself reminders

The following external reminders are also very simple, yet very effective. If you want to remember to make a phone call, turn the phone around or move it so that when you see the phone in a strange place you are reminded to make the call.

If you want to be sure to take things with you when you leave your home, simply place them by the front door beforehand so that you can't help but notice them when you leave. You've heard the expression, 'Out of sight, out of mind': place things in your sight and they will pop into your mind.

If you want to remember to walk the dog, simply imagine, vividly and with all your senses, your dog eating a giant watch. Then either tighten your watchband or wear your watch on the opposite wrist. The different physical sensation will keep you 'time aware', and you will connect watch with dog. After all, if you really saw your dog eating a giant watch it would be pretty memorable.

Stress and a hectic lifestyle are the enemies of memory. Each morning conduct a mental preview of the day and plan accordingly. If rain is predicted, put the umbrella by the door, or the chances are you'll forget it when you're running late for work and then you'll get caught in the rain! If you want to post a letter, either place it with your keys or put it by the door.

Being 'time aware' is also essential for many people, and yet often time slips by and another appointment is missed. If you're one of these people, buy a watch that beeps every half hour and you won't ever have an excuse for saying, 'Good grief, is that the time? I'm late for an appointment'. Activating your left brain, as shown on pages 32–3, will also help you become more aware of time.

If you've ever had milk boil over while you're watching television, next time put a cup or a saucepan on top of the television and you will be thinking about the milk non-stop.

Everyone benefits from using these simple methods for a week or two. This short period of making yourself remember helps focus attention (without tension), reduces absent-mindedness, lessens distractions and makes life much easier for both you and your family.

8

NUMBER-MUNCHING

It is quite possible for you to remember ten words in a row. You could for example string them along in a sentence, or use the MEALS technique. The words 'Sam, the naked man, running last, jokingly keeps falling behind' are easy to remember, but how did you go remembering the phone numbers or historical dates and facts in Chapter 1?

The untrained brain can lock into its memory banks between six and eight digits with a reasonable amount of effort. That's why for example, phone numbers are usually limited to around eight digits. If they were much longer Telecom's inquiry line would be working on overload! While the average person has an upper limit of seven to eight digits, in this chapter you will learn how to remember numbers of any length.

Take a few moments to recall any of the telephone numbers from Chapter 1.

The chances are you found it quite hard to remember those numbers just now, as most numeric information, unless regularly used, enters short-term memory only.

We've been learning that for our memories to be utilised correctly, we have to engage in whole-brain thinking. Unfortunately, numbers have very little meaning for most people. While 65 may bring images of retirement to your mind and 007 may trigger James Bond, it's harder to find meaning in 94792. In Chapter 6 you learnt a quick and easy way of remembering the numbers 1 to 99. Now that you are becoming increasingly competent with the MEALS technique you are ready to master a more advanced method for remembering numbers – one that is particularly useful for recalling strings of figures.

One of the tests you did in Chapter 1 involved pairing numbers with letters. While you may not know the pairs too well yet, they serve as a useful test of memory and will form the basis of any easy way to visualise numbers. The quiz appeared as:

6 sh; 4 r; 3 m; 8 f; 5 L; 1 t; 7 k; 9 p; 2 n; 0 s.

The more complete conversions, which we will be concerned with in this chapter, are as follows:

0 s, z; 1 t, d; 2 n; 3 m; 4 r; 5 L; 6 (the soft sounds) sh, ch,

Number-munching **97**

dg, j, g; 7 (the hard sounds) k, g, ck, c; 8 f, ph, v; 9 p, b.

We will now lock these into your memory, by ensuring we involve the limbic system and right brain.

I suggest you take advantage of how your eyes and brain co-ordinate. When you look upwards, you enhance your visual thinking abilities. If your eyes are level, you will find it easier to contemplate auditory (sound) thoughts, and looking downwards will help you contemplate tactile (touch) sensations. The word VAT may help you remember: Visual Auditory Tactile.

More specifically, to remember something you've:

- seen – look up to your left

- heard – look sideways to your left

- felt – look down to your right.

For previously unfamiliar:

- sights – look up to your right

- sounds – look sideways to your right.

Read each of the following paragraphs, and then use your multi-sensory perceptual abilities to lock in the numbers and the appropriate letter before moving on to the next idea.

EYES UP to contemplate a **3** falling over and becoming an **m**.

EYES LEVEL to say out loud, 'The Minnesota Mining and Manufacturing company is known as **3M** and I heard this on radio station **3MMM**'.

EYES DOWN to write the lower case **m** and be aware that it has **3** downstrokes in its formation.

Number-munching **99**

EYES UP	to contemplate a lower case **f** looking like a number **8** and a bright red **V8 F**ord.
EYES LEVEL	to say, 'I bought a **V8 F**ord at a **fete** for **8** cents'.
EYES DOWN	to write a lower case **f** and change it into an **8**.

EYES UP	to contemplate a **2** being rotated and flipped over to change into an **n**.
EYES LEVEL	to sound out '**2n, 2n**'.
EYES DOWN	to write the lower case **n** and feel the **2** downstrokes your hand makes in the process.

EYES UP	to see the word fou**R** with a capital **R** next to a **4**.
EYES LEVEL	to hear a golf-playing pirate yell, '**Fore! Aaarrgh**, me '**earties, fore!**'
EYES DOWN	to write the letter **r four** times.

EYES UP   to look at the back of your left hand as you have your fingers together and thumb sideways and notice that it forms the letter **L**.

EYES LEVEL   to say, '**5L, 5L, 5L, 5L, 5L**'.

EYES DOWN   to tap the fingers of your left hand on your lap to form again the capital **L**.

EYES UP   to notice that both the letters **t** and **d** have **1** downstroke and if the top of the number **1** slipped down it would change into the letter **t**.

EYES LEVEL   to hear that **t** and **d** rhyme as you say them **once**.

EYES DOWN   to feel your tongue behind your teeth as you say **t** and **d** and then write **d** and **t**, being aware that they have **1** downstroke.

EYES UP   to discover that the capital letter **K** is comprised of a number **7** on top of another **7**. You may also like to visualise a hard metal **cog** with **7** teeth.

EYES LEVEL	to say, '**7 cog, 7 cog, 7 cog**'.
EYES DOWN	to pick up the **7-kg cog**.

EYES UP	to see that **6** is the mirror image of a handwritten **j** with a completed loop in its tail.
EYES LEVEL	to say, '**Sex, shoosh**!'
EYES DOWN	to feel how your throat and jaw move when you say **sh, ch, j**.

EYES UP	to see that **9** is like **p** or **b**.
EYES LEVEL	to say, '**p** and **b** rhyme with **9**'.
EYES DOWN	to feel size **9 'pb** shoes' on your feet.

EYES UP	to see the word **zeros** starts with a **z** and ends with an **s**.
EYES LEVEL	to emphasise the **z** and **s** in the word **zeros**.
EYES DOWN	to write the word **ZooS**.

Perhaps you have noticed that only consonants are used as substitutes for numbers, with the vowels, a, e, i, o, u not being used.

Review all the possible conversions of digits into letters of the alphabet on pages 97–8, and give yourself a quick quiz to make sure that you are familiar with at least half of the conversions.

APPLYING THE TECHNIQUE

Now I would like you to picture for a moment an American Indian chief getting his feathers cut in a hairdressing salon. Do your best to introduce colour and movement in this scene.

You have concentrated on connecting the two images of Indian and hairdresser. If in an hour's time you were asked, 'Where was the Indian?', you would find it quite easy to reply, 'In a hairdressing salon'. If you were asked who was in the hairdressing salon, an Indian would pop into your mind.

If on the other hand you had to remember the address of a new hairdressing salon was 212 Main Street, you might be able to remember Main Street, especially if you were familiar with it, but you might find yourself wondering if the street number was 321, 121 or 212.

The simple way of remembering the correct street number is to change the number into a word that can then be visualised: 212 may, for example, be replaced by the appropriate letters, which are **n** (2 downstrokes), **d** or **t** (1 downstroke), and **n**. By saying this combination of letters either slowly or quickly you will find yourself saying 'n-d-n', and, if your eyes are level, the thought I**nd**i**a**n will most likely occur to you.

Usually, just by sounding out the letters that can replace a number, your will discover a word that you can use to lock in that number. If a word doesn't come to you quickly, you may find it easier, to begin with, if you methodically go through the different vowels that you can insert between the consonants.

HISTORY

If you were studying history and wanted to remember that Napoleon lost the vital battle of Waterloo in 1815, you would probably only need to lock in the digits 815. The three numbers can then be replaced by **f** or **v** for 8, **t** or **d** for 1 and **L** for 5. If after saying 'ftl' or 'vtl' quickly or slowly (with your eyes level) you don't immediately think of a word, simply begin to insert the vowels a, e, i, o, u. The first vowel, inserted in 'ftl', makes 'fatl', which becomes **fatal**. The third vowel, inserted in 'vtl' ('vitl'), suggests 'vital'. To lock in the year, simply visualise

Napoleon receiving the fatal blow to his hopes, losing the vital battle or even playing the **fiddl**e, if you prefer. If you wanted to go one step further, he eventually died in 1821 (when he became **faint**!).

To remember Beethoven was born in 1770, the combinations of letters could be: **c, k, s: g, g, s;** and so on. The words you could connect visually with Beethoven are **cakes, cooks, kegs, kicks, gags** ...

For 1905, the year of Einstein's theory of relativity, you could effectively use the idea of 'puzzle' to lock in 905.

One day a student in my seminar said he remembered the number/letter combinations more easily after creating the sentence with ten words in it that I quoted at the beginning of this chapter, '**S**am, **T**he **N**aked **M**an, **R**unning **L**ast, **J**okingly **K**ept **F**alling **B**ehind'. This is also a good way for you to remember the letter equivalents of the numbers 0 to 9 in order.

I suggest you return to page 2 and use these ideas to lock in the remaining historical facts and figures. It's vital that you practise on shorter numbers before you move to the following phone numbers.

Phone Numbers

We'll start off with the local **pizza parlour's** phone number, which you may remember is **74 1570**. By substituting the letters of the alphabet you are increasingly familiar with, we can change the numbers into an idea that can be processed through all the parts of your brain. To do this, visualise **pizzas** so huge that they are loaded onto a **cart**, which is then pulled along by gigantic **Legs**. Again, do your best to focus, even more than you have, on colour, sounds, smells and movement.

You've just learnt the phone number. After a quick review of that mental movie within 24 hours, whenever you need the phone number all you have to do is visualise pizzas and you are reminded of cart and Legs. Then it's a simple matter of ignoring any silent letters and vowels and converting the consonants into numbers to get c **7**, r **4**, t **1**; and L **5**, g **7**, s **0**.

Other words you could have used for 741 include card, grid, cord, court, karate, grate and carrot (we only say the 'r' sound once so there would only be one 4 in your number), and for 570 we could have used locks, lakes or logs. When starting off with this technique, it's better to use 'solid' words: words representing things that you are familiar with and could actually pick up or touch. For this reason, until you have been using the technique for a while, avoid words such as cried, carried or cared, and likes or looks.

We'll take another of the numbers on page 5 now. Visualise and lock in a kindergarten filled with **monkeys**

(3 27 0) scrambling up a gigantic **chisel** (605).

I suggest you begin by grouping the letters into threes to come up with an idea and then look for either longer or shorter words to fill in any gaps. For example, the phone number of your supermarket may become 'freezer lemon' (8404 532) or your local garage's phone number may be 'carpet buns' (7491 920). Make sure you firmly connect a descriptive image of the location of the number with your visualisation. Visualisations of monkeys/chisel or cart/Legs will be useless until you connect them with an image of the person or place whose number it is. Whenever you come to an impossible group of numbers, simply take the letters one or two at a time, rather than in larger blocks.

Now return to page 5 and use these techniques to remember the remaining phone numbers.

THE NUMTURE CONNECTION

If you choose, you can combine this letter-number system with your simple numtures from Chapter 6, to generate 1000 places in your mental filing cabinet. The following nine ideas represent the hundreds. They have been arrived at by using the letter–number system: the **t** of 'toe' has **1** downstroke, reminding you of the **1** in 100, the **n** of 'Noah' has **2**, reminding you of 200, and so on.

100	**t**oe
200	**N**oah
300	**m**ower
400	**r**ower
500	**L**aw
600	**j**aw
700	**k**ey
800	**f**ee
900	**p**ea

Should you ever need to remember 744, simply visualise a key (700) connected with a fork (44). In the same way, the number 316 could be a mower wrapped in tinsel.

USE IT AND IMPROVE IT

FOOD FOR THOUGHT

Remember when, as a child, you wouldn't be excused from the table until you'd finished your meal, and you used to try to hide that last piece of fish under your knife? Eating the crust on your sandwich was supposed to make your hair curly, and fish was supposed to make you brainy. All I can say is I must have been an expert at hiding my fish, as I was seriously considering starting my own elite group of thinkers called DENSA!

Perhaps you are enjoying a very successful life, yet do you realise that your most precious possession is your brain? For insurance purposes your car might be worth 25 000 dollars. If your brain was almost written off, you might reasonably expect a few million dollars.

And just in case you think it's too late for you to do anything about the quality of your brain, consider these

FACTS. **If your brain is adequately fed and exercised** throughout your life, in time you will be **more intelligent**, your **memory will be better**, and your **brain will be larger** than it is today! Even if you do nothing, it's likely that at eighty you will still have around 90 per cent of the brain cells you had in your youth. On the other hand, **if you abuse it you lose it**!

Whether you are young or old, or in between, you will benefit by acting on some of the suggestions that follow. While your brain comprises around 2 per cent of your body weight, it 'drinks' approximately 20 per cent of your blood, and burns two-thirds of your daily glucose needs.

Busy people still often light up a cigarette or have a strong cup of coffee to 'get their brain going'. Indeed some studies have shown that within seven seconds of lighting up, nicotine stimulates the production of some memory chemicals (neurotransmitters) in the brain, but the effects will only last for 15 to 30 minutes. Unfortunately nicotine is also used in insecticides and rat poison, so it may be better to engage in ten minutes of aerobic exercise each day, which will also stimulate the production of memory chemicals in the brain, and lessen the likelihood of cancer or heart disease.

Caffeine may also interfere with brain efficiency. Putting jet fuel in our mental Ferrari may increase its speed, but you can be sure that after a few laps the engine will seize! Caffeine is not a brain-booster. While it may stimulate the body, it is also believed to reduce the supply of blood to the brain. Heavy caffeine consumption may cause chronic fatigue. Moderate to high caffeine consumption is linked with poor academic performance, so perhaps you could substitute decaf or a piece of fruit or fruit juice for that cuppa. A big yawn will also increase the flow of oxygen to your brain and if you combine this with a 'King Kong' or 'Tarzan' exercise of thumping your chest, you will stimulate your immune system, activate your thymus, and increase your energy level.

Also, we often become dehydrated, so regular sips of water throughout the day are desirable. Plain water is preferable, as it is the only thing you can ingest that doesn't lower your mental energy by starting the digestion process. A piece of fruit will also usually be better than a processed food, and is a natural source of glucose, which the brain loves.

Nowadays more and more people are changing their lifestyles to improve their health, and yet most people fear losing their minds or going senile more than death. Alzheimer's disease is an underlying cause of death and ranks after heart disease, cancer and strokes as a leading cause of death. It used to be thought that Alzheimer's disease was a disease of old age, and yet more and more people in their forties and fifties are losing their memories. Either directly or indirectly, this situation will be experienced by one-third of Australian families. (However, forgetting where you've put something doesn't mean you're getting Alzheimer's disease; that's a 'normal' kind of forgetting, and you can acquire skills to overcome it.) Current research suggests that three factors may be involved in Alzheimer's disease: heredity, neuro-chemical deficiencies and environmental factors. While we can do nothing about the first factor it may be wise to counteract the other two factors.

In the same way that a correlation between smoking and cancer was put forward in the 1960s, people are now suggesting a link between aluminium and memory loss. If there is any imperfection in the workings of your brain, aluminium may accelerate the process. People who die as a result of Alzheimer's disease have large deposits of aluminium in their brain; they also have major deficiencies of a neurotransmitter by the name of acetylcholine.

If you are at all concerned about these risks it may be sensible to change to a low-aluminium deodorant and avoid antacids that are high in aluminium. Stainless steel or modern aluminium cookware with a non-stick surface may also be preferable to cook with.

Eating lecithin (especially if it contains phosphatides), or taking it as a supplement, is probably the easiest way to increase the production of acetylcholine in your brain, as it contains the key ingredient of choline. Fish is also a good source of choline, as are peanuts, soy beans, wheat germ, calf's liver and oatmeal.

Finally, it's vitally important you have a well-balanced diet and adequate food intake as you age. As elderly people are usually less active than they were in middle age, they tend to eat only two-thirds the quantity of a decade or two before. All too often there is not a great deal of variety in their diet, and their digestive system is not as effective as it once was. These three factors contribute to the sad fact that almost half our elderly relatives aren't getting their recommended daily allowances of essential vitamins and minerals.

The symptoms of a senile dementia include fatigue, forgetfulness, poor muscle co-ordination, irritability, depression and lethargy. Interestingly, these are also symptoms or malnutrition. Many people diagnosed as having Alzheimer's disease respond remarkably well when given a multi-vitamin supplement.

Remember the mottos 'use it and improve it' and 'abuse it and lose it' apply more to your brain and memory than any other aspect of your life.

SUMMARISING WHERE WE'VE BEEN
Before you develop your plan of action, let's briefly review where we've been together.

From the memory quizzes in **Chapter 1**, you began to learn about your brain's capabilities, and in **Chapter 2** discovered that your most important 'system' is your belief system. By regularly stimulating your neuro-vascular or emotional stress release points and using the 'Five-minute Fear Fix' you began to rid yourself of any unnecessary and incorrect ideas about who you are and what you can expect to achieve.

Chapter 3 gave you a simple user's guide to help you activate your brain through physical exercises and stimulate your thought processes via 'energy exercises'.

The brain-chain technique that **Chapter 4** gave you will prove very useful in remembering just about anything, from shopping lists to speeches and languages. Then there were the techniques given in **Chapter 5** for remembering people's names and faces that will help you relax with people and create more friends.

In **Chapter 6** you began to develop your mental filing cabinet (or database in this age of computers) and experienced 'whole-brain learning' to learn a list of chemical elements.

Chapter 7 contained some practical tips to improve your concentration and overcome absent-mindedness, while in **Chapter 8** you learnt how to remember facts and figures with ease, and 'steer' your eyes to enhance memory.

Finally, **this chapter** contained information about how you should care for your brain.

GETTING READY FOR ACTION

It's possible you've found this book stimulating and enjoyable reading, yet that is not my goal. I want you to become far more effective as a result of improving your memory and your mental skills. Is that your goal too?

Great! As soon as you can, visit a newsagent and buy a small packet of green self-adhesive dots. Have you ever bought a car or piece of equipment and then noticed, all of a sudden, that you see that model everywhere? On the principle that something out of the ordinary for you is foremost in your mind, over the next ten weeks, place those small green dots on your fridge, in your bathroom, in your car, on your wallet or handbag, at your desk, in fact anywhere you use your brain. Each time you see one of those green dots it will serve as a conscious and subconscious reminder to you to use the ideas contained in this book.

Review this book when you have your dots, and then you'll be ready for you action plan.

PUTTING IT ALL TOGETHER

Here's a timetable to help you improve your memory over a two-month period.

Week 1
Set yourself six daily goals and use the brain chain to lock them in. Dismantle a self-limiting memory each day and programme yourself for your future success.

Week 2
As above and activate your right brain upon waking each morning and again during the day. Utilise your energy exercises when appropriate.

Week 3
As above and use the techniques for remembering the names of people you meet, reviewing the names and how you remembered them in the evening.

Week 4
As above and learn and use your numtures for times, dates, and so on. Use the brain chain to lock them in. Review the numtures when you have any idle mental time such as while doing the dishes, waiting for public transport, vacuuming and gardening.

Week 5
As above and use the ideas for overcoming absent-mindedness.

Week 6
As above and practise memorising longer numbers, such as phone numbers, licence numbers, and your tax file number. Start by memorising your four-figure auto-teller card number if you have one.

Week 7
Make sure your eating habits are healthy, and throw out any antacids or indigestion mixtures that contain aluminium. Perhaps switch to a low-aluminium deodorant and cook with stainless steel, glass or modern aluminium cookware that has a non-stick surface. If you think it appropriate, cut down on fatty foods, caffeine, smoking and alcohol.

Week 8
Set your intermediate and life goals down on paper. Most people aim at nothing in life and hit their target with incredible accuracy! Ensure you enjoy one entirely new activity each month to stimulate your brain, and, most important of all, **remember that you are a great and marvellous creation** and deserve success in making the most of your vast mental resources.